GW00375244

STRAIGHT OUTTA BEING A LANDLORD

The UNFILTERED Reality of Owning A Rental Property

Kathe Michele Hamilton

May this content serve you well
as you take action toward achieving your goals.

For additional information about the author go to
www.KatheMichele.com

Dedication

To my daughter Kayla for never complaining about all the new business ventures I jumped into and being your own independent authentic self.

CONTENTS

Introduction 1

So here's the thing, if you're thinking about being a landlord for the first time or maybe you're currently a landlord and just want to co-sign with me on your landlord experiences. Well, then this is the book for you.

I've been an author for several years now and I write most of my books as a creative outlet to share my life experiences but most importantly to help other people navigate through the ups and downs of going after their dreams and goals.

I'm a pretty simple straightforward person and when I'm trying to learn something new or build capacity for others, I like easy reading and applicable examples. Hence, the reason why I wrote *Straight Outta Being a Landlord: The UNFILTERED Reality of Owning Rental Property*. I'm going to give you all the nitty-gritty information about <u>my personal experiences</u> of being a single, Black female landlord for three years in South Central Los Angeles, CA … during a pandemic!

Chapter 1: Full Transparency

I'M A RISK-TAKER! That's right, I said it out loud. It took me several years to admit it and might I add, I'm impulsive and impatient too, lol. Now, you wouldn't naturally think that I was a risk-taker since I am also a very quiet introverted person, but for some reason, I am able to manage all these shades of me in my life. Here's a little background information about me, so you can get a gist of who I was before I jumped into being a landlord.

I've been an educator for thirty years, an entrepreneur for fifteen years, and an author for seven years. Yeah, I consider myself a triple threat in my career paths. Even if it's just in my mind!

I say all this to say, once I set my mind to something ... I usually do it! Regardless of my knowledge, experience, or finances. The only experience I had prior to being a landlord was, buying a condo for myself in my 20s and buying a single-family home when I was married. Besides that, I didn't have a lick of experience before buying a rental property! I don't know if this risk-taker mentality is a bad quality to have or a good one, but it's a part of who I am. I'm trying to change the impulsive and impatient part but somehow it still tends to work out for me in the end ... knock on wood!

With that said, now you know what real estate knowledge and experiences I started with ...ZERO! This is how my mind works, I start everything with an idea and then I teach myself what I don't know along the way.

Lesson #1 (By the way, I'm going to be giving you lessons, tips, and examples throughout the book)

- *Don't be like me, and teach yourself **after** buying the property. Don't start doing or buying anything without EXTENSIVE research on property laws and management*
- *Pick the brain of other landlords with as many questions as you need to (treat them to lunch/dinner for their time)*
- ***Don't** get into real estate by yourself. Consider getting a business partner or silent partner*

Chapter 2: If You Don't Know, Now You Know

Picture it, sunny Los Angeles, CA in April 2019. I was strolling on Facebook and came across a post promoting an informational meeting about buying real estate. It piqued my interest because 1.) The people hosting it were African-American men 2.) The meeting was nearby and I was available 3.) I was financially comfortable and ready to buy a new home for my daughter and me to live in or mull over the idea of being a landlord. So I went and liked all the positive things that they presented.

I heard all the wonderful financial benefits of getting a home or rental property, the income stream, and the tax perks that come with being a landlord. No one had one negative thing to say. So a few weeks later, I contacted the presenters and began my journey to acquiring a rental property. The person I was working with assured me that this would be a great opportunity for me and that it would be no problem to hire their property management company so that I wouldn't have to deal with any tenant issues. I would just be collecting rent from the management company each month. **(Remember these words when we get to Chapter 6)**

It sounded like it was going to be easy like Sunday morning, right? Within a couple of months, I thought I had found the perfect property. It was a recently updated duplex. One unit had 2 Beds and 1Bath and the other had 3 Beds and 1 Bath. The smaller unit was empty and the bigger unit had tenants. The backyard space was very large and clean … (when I came to view the property). I put an offer in immediately without consulting a sole. In probably less than 24 hours, my offer was accepted and I suddenly felt excited and trapped at the same time!

- *Don't meet with any real estate agent or broker until you have assessed your long-term financial commitments*
- *Just like you shouldn't go to a car dealership alone, you shouldn't go to a real estate agent or broker alone*
- *Everyone DOES NOT have your best interest in mind when it comes to real estate. Get everything in writing. The goal of most agents and brokers is to make the most money from their sales commission*
- *Take pictures of the entire property the way it is before you buy it and be explicit about the condition it is to be sold to you versus when you viewed it.*

Ask yourself:

- *Will your discretionary funds or savings pay two mortgages/rent if needed?*
- *What impact will a change in your job have on your finances?*
- *What additional resources might you need for college tuition or long-term medical care in the future?*

Chapter 3: Location, Location, Location!

Make sure when you're looking for a rental property that it's in a location where you feel comfortable in yourself. Think about the type of tenants the neighborhood will attract. Let's keep it 100 %. If you have a property in a rough neighborhood, more than likely your tenants are probably going to be from that neighborhood too. Not saying everyone who lives in a rough neighborhood is going to be an undesirable tenant, but just be mindful of the neighborhood especially if you're not hiring a property management company. I managed my property alone for 2 years and never felt safe when I visited the property.

As you're visiting various prospective properties, don't be afraid to take notes, take pictures, or bring a checklist. Here are some of the little details that I overlooked during the process of buying a rental property:

- Number of steps and handrails: There are safety laws that require a handrail based on the number of steps.
- Windows and egress: There are safety laws that require windows to be large enough to escape out of in case of emergency.
- Door sweeps and deadbolts: There are safety laws that require you to have this on the front and/or back doors.
- Carbon monoxide and smoke detectors: Must be in multiple rooms.
- Gate and mailbox security: There should be some type of security if possible, especially in areas where crime and vagrants are an issue.

If you don't include these safety features in the selling process, then expect to pay for them yourself when the City Housing Authority decides to inspect your property for safety violations. Yeah, this also happened to
me a few months after buying the property. I got a few fix-it warnings or I'd have to pay a substantial fine!

Lesson #3

- *Be sure to check the property comps in the area and the average price other landlords are charging for rent*
- *Find out how much other landlords charge tenants for credit checks and/or applications*
- *Check how close the location is to a school. "Megan's Law" is important to know when you start screening for tenants*
- *You should know if the property is in a rent control area. This will dictate how much you can legally increase rent each year ... 3%, 4% 5%*

Notes: **13**

Chapter 4: The Price is Wrong … Bob!

So let's talk about the pricing, fees, and cost to actually run a rental property because if it doesn't make dollars it doesn't make sense. Also, you should have an idea of how much your agent and broker will make off of your sale. There's usually a flat percentage they get off any sale.

The first thing to consider is the price that you pay to buy the property. You base that on how much you can afford to pay each month. Make sure you get a compounded mortgage so that the property taxes and the mortgage are all wrapped into one monthly payment. You don't want to get a property tax bill later on down the line for like $2,000 twice a year. Also, aim for a monthly payment of at least $500 <u>below</u> what you really can afford. You must factor in additional monthly costs for the upkeep of the property. Here are some examples:

- Homeowners insurance fees
- City Housing yearly fees
- Pest control monthly fees
- Landlord monthly utility bills (landlords usually pay water, sewer, and/or trash bills)
- Lawn/tree care monthly bills
- Plumber services
- Handyman services

- *Get a good plumber and handyman as soon as possible. There were many things that the homeowner's insurance didn't cover that I needed to be done. It was faster to have my own maintenance people that I could call for a quick emergency.*
- *Keep an excel sheet record of all your expenses so that when it's tax time, it will be easy to find what can be a tax write-off.*
- *Attend all landlord and renter meetings that your city offers. You need to know all the laws and rights concerning your property.*
- *Don't jump into Section 8 Housing or Homeless Housing without getting ALL the facts and requirements for the program. All money, ain't good money!*

Chapter 5: What I Bought vs What I Got

Remember all those wonderful things I heard in the real estate meeting about buying a property? Well, I quickly learned the not-so-wonderful things about being a landlord as soon as I got the keys to the duplex.

Cue the "Sanford and Son" music in your head. When I went back to the rental property that I now own, I saw piles and piles of junk covering half of the large backyard of the duplex. The other half of the yard had an RV, a large storage trailer, and two cars. Trash was spilling out of the garbage cans, broken toys were scattered everywhere, and it looked like a small herd of kids were running a muck with no adult supervision. These my friends are the realities of being a landlord.

I had been hoodwinked, bamboozled, the old switcheroo, etc… The previous owner hid all the tenants' junk and extra kids during the selling process and then brought it all back after it was sold. Ain't that about a b_____!

Write your own rental agreement for your tenants or add an amendment, especially for these rules:

- Parking: If provided, only allow cars that have registered with the landlord. All others will be towed at their expense. No car washing allowed. (I actually put a lock on the outdoor spigots since I was paying the water bill.)
- Common Areas: Do not allow storage, dumping, tents, canopies, swing sets, adult-size plastic pools, or any kind of furniture beyond a <u>fold-up</u> outdoor chair and table. They are all a liability for safety reasons.
- Tenants: Be specific about how many people are allowed to live in the apartment. Two turns into six real easily if it's not in writing and enforced.
- Pets and hoarding: Believe it or not, there are some laws that protect these renter rights. Emotional support animals are protected. Some hoarding, which is sometimes considered a mental illness issue, is protected if it doesn't cause a safety hazard. Please thoroughly screen your tenants BUT be aware that you CAN' T ask potential tenants certain questions. Just like in a job interview. Do you research in your city or state to find out specifically what you can and cannot ask when vetting a tenant? (race, gender, kids, etc...)

Of course, I immediately contacted my realtors and they suggested I make the current tenants sign a new rental agreement stipulating the rules of dumping, cleanliness, and vehicles not allowed. I thought great, that would fix everything. All I have to do is tell the property management company that I was told would gladly manage my duplex for me right?

But wait, on top of all of this learning curve I was going through to be a landlord, then the COVID-19 pandemic hit! This brought on a huge set of new rental rights that all landlords whether they are big corporation landlords or single-building landlords like me, must abide by all the new COVID-19 pandemic rental laws. It was a nightmare in every way! Suddenly, tenants were allowed to break all of their rental agreement rules. Tenants could:

- Stop paying rent and don't need to worry about paying it back
- Move as many people into the apartment as they wanted
- Not be evicted for any reason

It was a renter's dream and a landlord's nightmare. I didn't know if I was going to die from Covid-19 or from a stroke due to the stress of no rent money coming in for an entire year. Luckily, I was able to put my mortgage loan into forbearance during that year and save my credit from tanking. I just had to "Let Go and Let God" on that one. The pandemic was beyond the world's control!

- *Read the current rental agreement thoroughly and consider removing all tenants as part of the selling process*
- *Stipulate the requirements of the condition of the property in order to purchase it ... in writing*
- *Observe the property during unscheduled appointments at all times of the day and night. Who's coming and going? What's the noise level? See how the tenants really live.*
- *Have a financial plan if tenants stop paying their monthly rent*

Notes:

_____
_____
_____
_____
_____
_____
_____
_____
_____
_____
_____
_____
_____
_____
_____
_____
_____
_____
_____
_____
_____
_____
_____
_____
_____

Chapter 6: Do It Yourself vs Hiring a Property Management Company

Don't believe the hype! That property management company that was hyped up to me and I was told I could hire them to run EVERYTHING for me … was suddenly not taking on any new properties. Yeah, a mouth drop moment for me. It hit me like a ton of bricks. Imma whole single Black female landlord by myself and not a clue of what to do or where to turn for help.

What have we been conditioned to do when we need help? Pray of course and then ask Google!
I Googled the heck out of the internet — how to be a landlord, rental agreements, California rental laws, renter's rights, landlord's rights, Section 8, and much more. All the things I should have done BEFORE buying rental property!

I even consulted a couple of property management companies. Some can be pretty pricey. The average rates were about $200-$400 a month. After a couple of months of trying to get my junkyard tenants to remove their stuff to no avail, I decided to consult with one of the property management companies for advice on evictions. They were very helpful and didn't charge me anything for asking questions. They even gave me a referral to their eviction attorney. What I learned from the eviction attorney was extremely eye-opening.

Evictions are a MF! They are helluva expensive. There are attorney fees, filing fees, and worst of all … you can't accept rent from the tenants you're evicting during the whole process. That's right you heard me!

Once you start the eviction process, you can not collect rent from a tenant you are trying to evict. After your case is processed and IF the judge makes a ruling in your favor, then you can collect rent. Oh and eviction cases can take anywhere from 1-6 months.
Suffice it to say, I gave up on my idea of evicting my junkyard tenants (3 years later, I paid a junk removal company $800 to haul most of it away and the tenants were eventually evicted by the new property management and now owners of the property).

Well, day by day I taught myself how to be a landlord and manage the property by myself for 2 years. Then, I allowed someone to manage it for me for a year. After feeling that freedom of not being tied to the property 24/7, I decided to sell the management company the duplex. It was the best decision for me to relieve the stress of being a landlord.

Here are some of the Pros and Cons of doing everything myself:

- Pro: All profits from the renters are solely yours. No monthly fee to a management company
- Pro: Learn what's really going on with your tenants and property
- Con: It intrudes on your personal life. Be ready for a fix-it call or complaint text at all times of the day and night (Don't give them your personal phone number. Use a Google number. My rookie mistake)
- Con: Dealing with stressful situations that might be dangerous by myself (Threats, robberies, tenant-to-tenant fighting, high police activity neighborhood)
- Con: Don't tell your tenants you're the owner of the property. Let them think you're just managing it. I feel like the tenants viewed me

  differently because I was a single Black female. Especially the male tenants. I don't believe they took my directives seriously and just saw me as a lady with very little authority to make them do anything.

- *Secure a property management company BEFORE you buy a rental property*
- *Do your due diligence to find a property management company that will meet ALL of your needs (maintenance and legal)*
- *Talk to other landlords to see if they are happy with their management services*

Bottom line, I think I've said it several times throughout the book now. I **HIGHLY suggest hiring a property management company**. It's worth the money to not have to deal with so many responsibilities when you're doing it alone. Perhaps if I had one at the beginning, I would still own the property.

I hope my unfiltered experiences, tips, and lessons gave you a behind-the-scenes look at some of the various issues that you may encounter if you become a landlord WITHOUT taking a serious deep dive into every aspect of the business.

My goal for this book was to provide guidance to those wild risk-takers like me that sometimes need someone to tell them to take a minute and be still so they can build their knowledge level first before taking on a new adventure.

Best of luck on your real estate journey!

For more books and online courses go to…

All books are available on www.Amazon.com

Make Money Teaching Cooking Classes:
A Guide to Start Your Own Kids Cooking Business

Workbook: Make Money Teaching Cooking Classes: A
Guide to Start Your Own Kids Cooking Business

Kid Entrepreneur: Don't Just Play The Game, Be The Game Changer

Teen Entrepreneur: Don't Just Play The Game, Be The Game Changer

Parents as Partners Planner: It Takes A Village

Retirement Journal

Allergy Tracker Journal

My online courses:

https://sidehustlecollege.teachable.com

Printed in Great Britain
by Amazon

30835380R00021